BEES AND HONEY

Table of Contents

Short History of Honey

Honey has been around f or just as long as one can remember life. Historians have proof that honey bees existed more than 150 million years ago through the fossils found and dated. Paintings found in Spain's caves about 7,000 BC show that bees and honey were quite common. Records of bees were also discovered in the Sun Temple of Cairo dated about 2,400 BC.

For Egyptians, honey was only for royalty, which explains why jars of honey were retrieved from the tombs of pharaohs. They called it; "the nectar of gods." by the way, the honey thus retrieved, which was easily thousands of years old was still unspoiled and healthy to eat. The Romans too looked at honey as a divine food, and it was offered to gods and royalty.

Beekeeping was a prominent and respected occupation throughout the Roman Empire. Besides using it as food, the Romans used it for treating wounds during wartime and during peacetime for making wine, which was called mead.

The Greeks saw honey as medicine as well as delicious food. There are records of many recipes dating back to the 5th Century that show honey as the main ingredient for many types of cakes, cheesecakes, and sweetmeats.

Post the establishment of Christianity, the popularity and demand for honey increased exponentially owing to the requirement of candles in the churches across Europe. Honey was used as the primary sweetening agent until late 17th century when sugar gradually took over.

It's amazing to note the bees' ability to adapt and survive over the years and across the globe. You can find honeybees thriving in regions from the equator right up to the Arctic Circle. In fact, you will find honey bees wherever man lived right from the beginning of time until the present.

THE DIFFERENT TYPES OF BEES

In this context, the term "race" refers to the type of bees, which adapted to their geographical area. There are ten types of honey bees plus one hybrid type, i.e. the Africanized honey bee. Here are few of the most common honey bee species:

The Italian Bee

It's a variation of bee species that can be recognized by the 4-5 bands that line its abdomen. The Italian bees are gentle to manage, which makes them very popular with beekeepers. They lay low in winter and build up very quickly in the spring. The downside to these bees is that they tend to increase in swarming.

Caucasian Bee

This species of bees owe their name to their origin, i.e. the Caucasus Mountains situated between the Caspian Seas of Russia and the Black Sea. These bees are gray in color, very hard working and gentle to handle. They tolerate the winter cold well and in the spring build slowly, with a low tendency for swarming. The Caucasian bees are known to be the highest producers of propolis. The downside here is that this species is susceptible to Nosema and other similar diseases.

Carniolan Bee

This species of bees is found in North Yugoslavia, Australian Alps and Danuble Valley. They are gentle to handle, and their body is smaller than the other species and has dull-greyish color. Similar to the Italian bees, they lay low in the winter and breed very quickly in the spring, which gives them a tendency to swarm.

The German Bee

This species of bees are the original type brought in by the early settlers to the Western countries. Their body is dark colored, large, and they winter well. These bees are aggressive when interfered with and very nervous when on the comb. They breed slowly and are less hard working than other species of bees.

The Buckfast Hybrid Honey Bee

This bee species was created by a monk from Buckfast Abbey - Brother Adam – hence, the name. The bees have been bred to be gentle, highly productive and made resistant to tracheal mites.

The Russian Honey Bee

This variety originates from the Primorsky region. They were produced specially for building resistance against parasites. They are defensive, but oddly they do not sting much, choosing rather butt with their heads. They are productive, but other traits are not fixed.

The Africanized bee

This variety is found in Southern and Western America. They are nicknamed as killer bees because they are horribly aggressive. They are known to chase those who they attack for a quarter mile before giving up.

One thing is for sure, though: each bee group forms a colony. Honeybees live in colonies that beehive owners strive to maintain, feed, and transport for pollination. The beekeeper first provides a beehive to be a home for the colony. This structure is created in a way that can enable honeybees to lay down their waxed honeycombs where they store honey and raise their broods.

THE COLONY

Colony consists of one queen, a few drones (male bees) and a significant population of infertile female bees (worker bees). A single mid-summer colony can have forty thousand to eighty thousand bees.

The Queen – She is the biggest bee in a colony. The Queen is picked up by the worker bee from her larvae stage. She eats Royal jelly, a milky secretion released from the glands found on the heads of young worker bees. So she becomes sexually mature over time. When the queen bee comes out of her cell, she mates while in flight with thirteen to eighteen drones.

The mating gives her millions of sperm cells, which remain on her for the entire life (2 to 5 years). Her work afterward is to produce more worker bees. She can lay up to three thousand eggs every day if she is well-nourished and healthy. The queen bee is always surrounded by young worker bees while she lays her eggs. Their work is to feed her and clean her.

Drones – These are big-eyed bees that look bigger than the worker bees. They do not sting, surprisingly. Drones are brawny-bodied bees, but they have to be swift enough to catch with the queen when she comes out to mate. Their big eyes enhance their vision so that they can spot the Queen. They live for ninety days only and in severe winter, they are forced out of the hive.

Worker bees – These are the infertile females who do the entire load of donkey work. In summer, ninety-eight percent of the hive's population is made of worker bees. And in winter, the colony has only the queen and worker bees. Their work is to feed the queen and her broods, guard the beehive entrance, improvise a fan with their wings and collect nectar. They also produce the wax for sealing the honeycombs.

HOW HONEY IS CREATED?

Honey is the food for bees. They generate this food to keep themselves alive during winter when flowers disappear, and they cannot gather nectar any longer. Honey is made through a complex process. It starts with the honey bee collecting nectar from various flowers.

The honey bees have a special "pouch" where the nectar is stored after it is ingested, which is called "honey stomach." When the nectar reaches this pouch, it is mixed with invertase or bee enzyme, which transforms the sugar in the nectar into glucose (dextrose) and fructose (levulose) – both, certain sugars or monosaccharides.

This process commences as soon as the honey bee ingests the nectar. By the time the insect has reached home, the nectar mix is passed on from the forager honey bee to the house honey bee from mouth to mouth. The house bees, in turn, regurgitate the nectar mix into the honeycomb after which they fan it by rapidly moving their wings to eliminate whatever moisture left in it.

When the bees feel all the moisture has gone, and the honey is just right, they cap it. It's usually the sign that beekeepers are looking for so they can collect some of the honey. Why honey never spoils is still a mystery. It could be attributed to the fact that the processing of honey also produces gluconic acid which is a natural preservative. This compound is responsible for maintaining the pH of the honey at a level where no bacteria, fungi or any other micro-organisms can grow.

By definition, it just means honey that has not been pasteurized. The next question, normally would be, "What is pasteurized honey?" Honey that is not heated above 35 degrees Celsius (95 degrees Fahrenheit) is not pasteurized. The honey bees themselves keep the honey at about 35 degrees – and at this level, the honey is alive. In other words, the beneficial organisms, enzymes, etc. are all alive.

When the honey is heated above this temperature, the beneficial ingredients are killed transforming honey to something very much comparable to artificial sweetener. It's why it's important to use raw honey exclusively.

Pure Honey versus Raw Honey

The term "raw honey" means not only not being heated beyond 35C or 95F degrees but also that it is consumed as it is picked from the hive. In other words, the honey would be consumed along with bits and pieces of everything that might "fall" into it while it is made and these would be bee parts (legs, joints, etc.), royal jelly, propolis, pollen and beeswax among others.

Most people do not feel comfortable with the idea of consuming honey bee and honeycomb debris along with the honey, and hence, they prefer to have it strained. Straining the raw honey would remove all the bits and pieces described above leaving behind the honey that we know, i.e. deep golden-yellow, viscous and sweet. It's raw honey in the real sense of the word.

The raw honey would still contain a large amount of pollen since it is fining than the cloth mesh and also retain all the beneficial organisms, as intended by the bees.

Pure honey, on the other hand, is filtered. The modern process of filtering involves force-presses, which pushes the honey through certain material/ barrier to remove everything from it. When this is done, slight pressure is added to it to ensure that it gets through relatively quickly.

It results in an increase of heat, which is way above the 35C/95F degrees – hence, the honey becomes pasteurized. Filtering is typically done for large-scale commercial operations, where honey is being bottled in large numbers for sale. The process, which is mechanized, makes honey lose almost all of its benefits because it kills the living organisms/ nutrition it contained.

What is Organic Honey?

By definition, organic honey is the honey made from organically grown flowers. By definition, it sounds simple; in reality, it's is not. It is not easy to prove or control where the bees forage for nectar. Bees can fly up to 8 km or 5 miles in search of flowers. It is not very easy to establish that ALL the flowers in an 8 km radius are organically grown.

The Africanized bees can, if required, fly up to 80 miles foraging for flowers. Hence, it is almost impossible to guarantee fully that the honey any beekeeper collects is 100 percent organic, even if they have the largest of all beekeeping farms.

The best way to buy raw honey is right from the beekeepers or farmers' markets since these markets have rules about the maximum distance radius for an origin of the products, it might be easy to find a beekeeper who sells his honey at these markets. The honey that is mass-packed by large companies is flash heated and micro-filtered, which means that you are buying "dead" honey bereft of any benefits.

THE PRESENTATION OF HONEY

Honeybees spend their lifetime building replacement honeycombs rather than making extra honey. And to produce one kilogram of beeswax, which is used to repair and seal honeycombs, worker bees must eat seven pounds of honey.

Because of how they consistently maintain their honeycombs, man can harvest the most distinctive forms of honey. In this section, we will outline many types of honey that you can eat.

Raw honey - A settling tank kept at room temperature is used to extract and clean this honey. It contains almost all the good things that bees gather from nature. Raw honey will form granules much faster, though, and when put in a jar the liquid fructose might isolate itself on top and the granular glucose on the base of the container.

Liquid Pasteurized Honey – This honey is extracted and cleaned with flash heating. It is heated to a very high-temperature range and then it is filtered well through a one to five-micron filter and then cooled very fast. As a result, of high heating, liquid pasteurized honey loses its organic beauty. It is, however, the only type of honey that will not granulate before nine months.

Honeycomb – This is usually reserved for people who like to consume the entire bee's product. Honeycomb is typically untouched by human hands and contains all the healing properties of honey. Honeycombs are chewed, though, and some people do not like it.

Liquid Honey (filtered) – This is the sort of honey that is already extracted and cleaned with the 50-micron filter. Then it is heated to the temperature found in the hive on a hot day is attained. This honey has every right thing that the bee gathers from nature. In about two to six months, the liquid honey will crystallize, but this will depend on the nectar it was made from.

Creamed Honey/Whipped Honey - This type of honey is made from the organic liquid honey, and it is granulated in a controlled crystallization process. It forms uniform crystals, and so it results in a smooth, creamy consistency like that of butter or jelly.

Cut Comb or Liquid-Cut Comb - This is liquid honey with some chunks of the Honeycomb put in a jar.

BENEFITS OF USING HONEY

Honey today is primarily used as food more than anything else. However, honey is also a medicine since it has antifungal, antibacterial and anti-viral properties.

Raw honey consists of phenylethyl caffeate, caffeic acid, methyl caffeate, phenylethyl dimethyl caffeate and some other phytonutrients, which have anti-tumor and anti-cancer properties.

Cholesterol, High Blood Pressure, and Obesity

According to Ayurveda honey can remove fat from all tissues in the body. Add about ten drops of apple cider vinegar and one teaspoon of honey to a glass of water. It will help you lose weight, reduce bad cholesterol, and regulate blood pressure.

Hay Fever Attack

Chewing on a honeycomb is known to cure attacks of hay fever. To prevent it altogether, mix honey and bee pollen in 2:1 ratio and have one teaspoon daily. It will build immunity against it.

Sore Throat

You have a sore throat for any reason (cold, or having spoken for too long)? Add one teaspoon of honey and one teaspoon of lemon juice to a glass of warm water. Drink 3-4 times daily.

Energy Booster

Whenever you feel, fatigued take a little honey for an instant pick-me-up. It's excellent for people who work long hours, over-active or over-stressed (with studies) kids and convalescing people.

Home Remedy

Honey is a living food as explained earlier. It is paramount that you use RAW honey exclusively. The mass-bottled honey, which has been machine filtered is dead and is more harm than help since everything that is good has been killed by the pasteurization process.

In ancient India, Egypt, and many other civilizations, raw honey has been recognized and highly revered for its medicinal properties. Here are a few highly efficient and straightforward remedies you can make at home:

Oral Ulcers

Mix a pinch of turmeric (Curcuma longa) with one teaspoon of honey and apply gently to the ulcerated area. That will make you salivate and expel toxins. Do not swallow the spit; spit it out to help with the healing process.

Internal Ulcers

Mix one teaspoon of honey in a cup (250 ml) warm milk. Add a pinch of turmeric and drink at least twice daily.

Asthma and Respiratory Distress

Honey is excellent for respiratory distress. Take a small glass bowl and mix one teaspoon of honey, ¼ teaspoon of pippali (Piper longum) and ½ teaspoon of bay leaf (Laurus nobilis) powder 2-4 times a day for almost instant relief.

Hiccups

You can make your own natural anti-spasmodic medicine with honey. Take a small glass bowl and mix castor oil and honey in equal proportions (1:1 ratio). Dip your finger or a teaspoon in the mix and lick very slowly. The hiccups will stop.

Smoking

Do You want to quit smoking? Honey can help you. An add1/2 teaspoon of honey to small cubes of pineapple and chew a few before you light a cigarette. Gradually, your craving for cigarettes will disappear.

Stomach Ache

Take a small glass bowl and mix in it one teaspoon honey, a 1/4th spoon of celery (Apium graveolens) seeds and 1/4th teaspoon ground bay leaf. Have this mix before every meal.

Chronic Fever

To cure, chronic illness makes a cup of tea with holy basil (Ocimum tenuiflorum) leaves (use about 10-15 per cup or 1 teaspoon of basil leaves powder). Add to it one teaspoon of honey and 1/4th teaspoon of freshly powdered black pepper.

Poor Blood Circulation

Heat 1½ cup of water and add to it a 1/4th teaspoon of trikatu, one teaspoon of cinnamon (Cinnamomum Verum) and one teaspoon of honey. Steep for about 8-10 minutes. Take this mix 2-3 times per day.

Anxiety

Mix a pinch of nutmeg powder and one teaspoon of honey in a cup of freshly squeezed orange juice. Drink it 2-4 times daily.

Sinus Congestion

Mix equal amounts of ginger juice and honey and have 2-3 times a day for about 4-7 days.

Common Cold

Mix equal amounts of honey and ginger. Add to it ½ teaspoon cinnamon powder. Take this combination three times daily.

Open Wounds

Raw honey is an excellent antibiotic and disinfectant. Add honey to sterilized gauze and apply to the wound. Bandage the area to prevent the dressing from falling or moving. Use in the morning; change it at night before you go to sleep.

Arthritis Pain

Take a small glass bowl and mix 200 grams of guggul with two teaspoons of honey. Take this combination 2-3 times a day.

Insomnia

Take 1-2 teaspoons of honey at bedtime. You will not only have an excellent sleep but also lose weight as honey will trigger fat loss while you sleep.

You can also add two teaspoons of honey to a cup of warm milk and take it before you go to bed. Prepare a chamomile tea and add to it 1-2 teaspoons of honey. Sip it at bed time for a guaranteed good sleep.

Immune System Booster

Honey is very effective in strengthening your immunity system. Warm a glass of water and add to it two teaspoons of lemon juice and two teaspoons of honey. Take this first thing in the morning. Do not consume anything for 45 minutes after that. It will not only boost your immune system but also trigger fat loss and help you lose unwanted weight.

Green tea with cinnamon powder and honey also boosts the immune system.

Bad Breath

Take ½ glass of warm water and add to it one teaspoon of honey and ¼ teaspoon cinnamon powder. Gargle with this natural breath freshener to enjoy fresh breath through the whole day.

Cancer

Some studies have pointed that honey possesses anti-tumor and anti-carcinogenic properties. Taken regularly, honey can help prevent or at least significantly lower the risk of cancer.

Antiseptic

Honey is an excellent remedy for infections. It can be used for treating candida infection, athlete's foot, burns, cuts, mosquito bites, insect bites, scrapes, and bruises, etc. Honey possesses anti-pyritic, anti-inflammatory and mildly analgesic properties.

Hangover

Did you party for too long last night? Here is a magic recipe that will remove all the signs and bring you back to earth after a hangover. Take a glass and add 70 ml of yogurt, 80 ml of orange juice and 15 ml (3 teaspoons) of honey.

Create a paste with cinnamon and honey and apply it to the aching tooth. The pain will decrease considerably.

It is important to mention that though each recipe is tried and tested before being presented here, it's recommended to use the remedies ONLY after consulting your medical practitioner.

USING HONEY FOR WEIGHT LOSS

The Hibernation Diet

The hibernation diet is a boon for those who hate any restrictions in their lifestyle or exercise regimes. Of course, it advocates healthy dieting and moderating refined foods, but it does not have many hard and fast rules. What you have to do is take two teaspoons of honey at night just before you sleep.

You can have the honey right out of the jar, straight, without mixing anything with it or you can have it with a little warm milk. The honey and the sleep will then work together and consume the fat in your body. You will lose pounds as you sleep – doing nothing more.

Miraculous? Remarkable? Wow? Yes, to all that. And yes, it works, too.

Owing to the 1:1 fructose to glucose ratio honey enables the production of hormones and burning of fat. An in-depth study -on this premise was published in the April 2004 issue of The Journal of Medicine explains it quite quickly. The 1:1 ration is the secret. It seems that all sugar is stored in the liver, where with the help of fructose it's processed and then released in the blood.

Typically, the body should be burning 70% fat while sleeping. That can happen only when the liver is fueled and does not need to work further to process sugar into glucose. It's where honey does the trick. With the full liver, the body gets into "repair mode" at night, during rest. Part of the repair process is burning fat. It is what happens in "hibernation" – hence, the name.

Lemon and Honey Weight Loss Recipe

The lemon and honey recipe is an age-old weight loss remedy tried and tested for generations. It's perhaps one of the easiest ways to lose weight. It involves drinking a glass of hot water with 2-3 spoons of honey the first thing on waking up in the morning.

You might not eat or drink anything after drinking this mix for about 45 minutes. After this period, you can have your breakfast as you normally do.

Cinnamon and Honey Weight Loss Recipe

The cinnamon and honey recipe is easy to make and use, and it gives some of the most amazing results. To make the recipe, you will need 1 cup of boiling water, one teaspoon of freshly ground cinnamon powder and one teaspoon of honey.

Mix the cinnamon thoroughly with the boiling water and set it aside too steep for about 15-30 minutes. The longer you leave it, the thicker in consistency it would become. If you prefer yours, a little thinner cut down the steeping time.

Add the honey when the water is cold enough. Too hot and you would kill all the beneficial living organisms in the honey. Drink these components first thing in the morning, on an empty stomach. Do not drink or eat anything after that for about 30-45 minutes.

The apple cider vinegar and the honey mix work in the same manner as lemon and honey works. Take a glass of water and mix in 2 teaspoons of honey and 1 or ½ teaspoon of apple cider vinegar. Have this combination 2-3 times a day.

A lot of information advocating this folk medicine is found in Dr. DC Jarvis, who wrote the famous book, "Folk Medicine" in 1958. Besides aiding weight loss, this great mix also helps with many other health conditions such as eczema, cholesterol, high blood pressure, arthritis, halitosis (bad breath), brittle nails, heartburn, food poisoning, obesity and premature aging.

A word of warning – do not use commercial distilled vinegar for this remedy. Instead buy raw and unfiltered apple cider vinegar – ensure it has "mother," which is proof that the vinegar is alive. Honey, of course, must be raw and unpasteurized.

ANOTHER AWESOME USES OF HONEY

The Mead

In the simplest definition, mead is nothing but honey and water. When water is added the high content of sugar makes it easy to trigger fermentation following which a particular wine is produced, called mead. The honey needs to consist of at least 20% moisture to start the fermentation process.

There are two types of mead you can make, i.e. dry and sweet.

Using it in Cooking

Honey is a common ingredient in the kitchen, and you will find many world-famous chefs recommending its use in the kitchen. When cooking with honey, it would be good if you pay attention to the following tips.

Don't worry, this is not a problem; and no, the honey is not false. Pure honey does crystallize. To get it back, take water in a pan and bring to a boil. Remove from heat. Pour the honey into a bowl and then place that bowl in the pan of boiling water. As the water cools, the honey will liquefy.

Easy Measuring

If you want to measure honey, spray a little olive oil on the measuring container so, the honey does not stick in. To accurately measure a cup, use a 12 oz jar.

USING HONEY FOR BEAUTY

Honey is an excellent beauty aid because:

1. It has anti-bacterial and anti-inflammatory properties, which also prevents degeneration of skin and promotes regeneration.
2. It can enhance collagen production and hence, treats scars and other marks on the skin.
3. It is a humectant, i.e. it not only retains moisture but also attracts it. That makes honey an excellent moisturizer.

Here are a few simple remedies that could work wonders when included in your beauty regime. Because honey has no side effects and is a magnificent disinfectant and healer, as long as you're okay you are using the real thing. Ensure that you use these remedies at least 2-3 time a week; also, it should be applied consistently for about 3-6 weeks before you see any real results.

Acne Treatment

If you suffer from acne honey could become one of your greatest allies. What I suggest you to do is massage a little on the face and leave it for 15-25 minutes. Clean with above average water and feel the difference on your skin.

To shrink/ dry the acne take a small glass bowl and mix in it two tablespoons of honey with a ½ teaspoon of newly squeezed lemon juice. Massage this mix on your face and leave it for 20-30 minutes; wash it off with warm water. That disinfects the skin and moisturizes it was killing the existing acne and prevents new ones from forming.

Mix 3 tablespoons of honey with a one teaspoon of freshly Massage this mix on your face and leave it for 20-30 minutes. Massage this mix on your face and leave it for 20-30 minutes; wash it off with warm water.

Mix 1 tablespoons of honey with finely ground oats. Apply to face and leave it dry for about 20-30 minutes. It will help with exfoliation of the skin, fight acne and keep the face soft and moisturized. It's also an excellent scrub for the face, in case you need to try it out.

Face Scrub

Mix 2 tablespoons of finely ground almond with one tablespoon honey to make a smooth paste. Add to it ½ teaspoon of lemon juice. Massage this mix on your face and wash it off with warm water.

Mix ½ teaspoon of sea salt with 2-3 tablespoons of honey to make a smooth paste. Massage this mix on your face and wash it off with warm water.

Face Wash

Mix 2 tablespoons of honey with a ½ teaspoon of rose water/ milk and a pinch of sandalwood powder. That makes a cold face wash that will leave the skin of the face moistened and feeling fresh.

Honey is an excellent ingredient for face packs. Here are a few you could try out immediately.

For oily skins and pimples treatment – mix in 1:1 ratio honey and Fuller's earth. Massage this mix on your face and leave it for 20-30 minutes; wash it off with warm water. Apply a natural moisturizer.

For refreshing tired skin and anti-tan pack – mix one tablespoon of honey with two tablespoons of grated cucumber and one teaspoon of milk. Massage this mix on your face and leave it for 20-30 minutes; wash it off with warm water. It will leave the skin smooth and without blemish.

For smooth and sensational skin – mix two tablespoons of honey with a ½ teaspoon of glycerin and two pinches of turmeric. Massage this mix on your face and leave it for 20-30 minutes; wash it off with warm water. You will find your face glowing.

4.   Bleaching – take a ripe tomato and two tablespoons of honey and ran them through the blender to make a thick paste. Massage

this mix on your face and leave it for 15-20 minutes; wash it off with warm water.

5.   Bleaching and moisturizing – mix in 1:1 ratio papaya paste and honey. Massage this mix on your face and leave it for 20-30 minutes; wash it off with warm water.

6.   Glowing blemish-free skin – mash one ripe banana and mix with 2-3 tablespoons of honey in a bowl. Massage this mix on your face and leave it for 10-20 minutes; wash it off with warm water. It will gradually remove all blemishes from your face.

Anti-Aging Face Pack

Honey, oatmeal, and yogurt – mix in 1:1 proportion honey, yogurt, and grain to make a smooth paste. Massage this mix on your face and leave it for 20-30 minutes; wash it off with warm water.

Honey and onion juice – for preventing wrinkles, this is an excellent remedy. Mix two teaspoons of honey and two teaspoons of onion juice. Massage this mix on your face and leave it for 20-30 minutes; wash it off with warm water.

Honey and egg – to lighten the color of your skin, use a mix of 2-3 tablespoons of honey with a raw egg. Massage this mix on your face and leave it for 20-30 minutes; wash it off with warm water.

Instant Face Rejuvenator

Take one tablespoon of honey, ½ teaspoon of lemon juice and one tablespoon of egg white. Massage this mix on your face and leave it for 20-30 minutes; wash it off with warm water.

Hair Treatment

Mix 100 grams (4 oz) honey with 50 grams (2 oz) extra virgin olive oil. Massage into the scalp thoroughly and ensure that it coats the hair. Wrap a warm towel around your head and leave it for 15-20 minutes. Wash hair frequently.

Hair Bleach

Mix 1 teaspoon of honey with one teaspoon of freshly squeezed lemon juice. Apply on the hair in the direction of growth. Leave for 10-15 minutes and rinse.

Mix 1 tablespoon of honey with one teaspoon of beeswax granules and ½ teaspoon olive oil. Add to it 2-4 drops of rose water. It makes excellent hand cream for winter or dry seasons.

HEALTH INFORMATION

Honey is attributed with a long list of health benefits among which are:

Nutrition Information

Serving Size: 1 regular cup (339 gram)

Percent Daily Values are based on a 2,000-calorie diet).

Calories	1031	4317kJ
Carbohydrates		
Total Carbohydrate	279g	93%
Dietary Fiber	1g	3%
Starch	--	
Sugars	278g	
Fats and Fatty Acids		
Total Fat	0.0g	
Protein	1g	
Vitamins		
Vitamin C	1.7mg	3%
Riboflavin	0.1mg	8%
Niacin	0.4mg	2%
Vitamin B6	0.1 mg	4%
Folate	6.8mcg	2%
Vitamin B	120.0mcg	0%
Pantothenic Acid	0.2mg	2%
Choline	7.5mg	
Betaine	5.8mg	
Minerals		
Calcium	20.3mg	2%
Iron	1.4mg	8%

Magnesium	6.8mg	2%
Phosphorus	13.6mg	1%
Potassium	176mg	5%
Sodium	13.6mg	1%
Zinc	0.7mg	5%
Copper	0.1mg	6%
Manganese	0.3mg	14%
Selenium	2.7mcg	4%
Fluoride	23.7mcg	
Sterols		
Cholesterol 0mg	0.0mg	0%
Phytosterols	0.0mg	0%
Water	58.0g	

[1] http://nutritiondata.self.com/facts/sweets/5568/2

MYTHS ABOUT HONEY

With honey being around for thousands of years, it 's okay to uncover some myths about it, which would prevent you from enjoying the benefits of this wonderful super food. Below are a few of the most famous ones exploded.

Myth 1: You should never use a metal spoon with honey as this will spoil it.

The Truth: While it is true that honey will corrode an iron spoon, the new spoons are made of stainless steel. There is no fear of stainless steel becoming oxidized; hence, there is no harm done here.

Myth 2: Do not mix honey in cold water; hot water is best for this.

The Truth: While it is true that honey mixed with warm water is highly beneficial to the digestive system, drinking it in cold water is okay too. There is no harm or hard and fast rule for drinking it either way.

Myth 3: If the honey crystallizes, it is not pure; or it has gone bad and needs to be discarded.

The Truth: Pure honey crystalizes. Nothing is wrong with crystallization or the honey after crystallization. Do not throw your honey away just because it has crystallized. It does not affect the nutritional value or health benefits of the honey.

Myth 4: Honey never spoils; even when you forget to close the lid.

The Truth: The "never get spoiled" property is valid, but only if the moisture remains at the minimum. If you leave the lid open, and there is enough moisture in the air, the honey will get spoiled.

Myth 5: Honey is available in both liquid and powder form.

The Truth: Honey does not come in powder form. Many confuse the cactus honey powder with bee honey. The cactus honey powder is a product derived from the juice of the Agave cactus plant that mostly grows in Mexico. Honey from bees comes in liquid form.

Myth 6: Honey contains fat and eating too much of it can have you gain weight.

The Truth: Honey does not contain FAT at all. You can have as much honey as you want. There are no bad side effects from eating honey.

Myth 7: The amber color liquid honey is the best to consume. The raw honey comes with too many impurities to be healthy.

The Truth: This is one of the most harmful myths because it makes you buy and consume the "dead" honey. The honey you find in jars in supermarkets look more impressive and attractive. However, it is the raw honey that is "alive" and hence, beneficial to you. The things you see floating in the raw honey would be pieces of comb, bee pollen and even bee legs. It will tell you that the honey is pure.

CONCLUSION

Honey is one of the most versatile superfoods mankind knows today. Besides being a meal by itself, honey comes with tremendous health benefits. This is something that should be on everyone's kitchen shelf. Not only it can help you with a wide variety of ailments, but also assist you with your beauty regime.

It is very easy to see why honey is a hot favorite the world over. There is almost no limit to how you can use it, cooking, beauty, health, weight loss and so many others and it goes without saying, it is tasty and easy to store. If not exposed to humid air, it can last forever. Jars of honey recovered from the Egyptian Pharaoh's were opened after 2,000-3,000 years – and the honey was still edible.

It is important to note that the honey you need to use is the raw one. The pasteurized honey sold in supermarkets will most likely be adulterated, besides being dead and hence no use to your health. The best buy is right from the beekeepers or farmers farm; the worst is what you find on the shelves of the supermarkets.

RECIPES

Whether giving a beautiful glaze to your steak, putting a buzz in your morning breakfast, or drizzled over dainty cakes, a spoonful of this amazingly sweet nectar is sure to turn your meals into masterpieces.

Honey is such a versatile cooking ingredient with a unique flavor that adds a magical touch to almost all foods – puddings, desserts, barbecue meats, homemade cookies, pastries, cakes, salad dressings, etc.

Honey recipes in this book, such as honey granola, honey apple Bundt cake, Savory Honey-Garlic Steaks, and cinnamon honey butter, show just how versatile honey can be. Enjoy our collection of amazing honey recipes today and find out what all the buzz is about.

Ingredients

- 150g honey
- 100g sultanas
- 100g wheat germ
- 100g dried apricots
- 150g dates
- 100g hazelnuts
- 150g sunflower seeds
- 100g bran
- 250g rolled oats
- 60ml groundnut or sunflower oil

Directions

Preheat your oven to 350°F.

Heat oil and honey in a pan until honey is melted.

Mix sunflower seeds, bran, and oats in a bowl. Add the honey mixture and mix well.

Transfer the mixture to a baking tray and roast for about 25 minutes turning the mixture about 4 times.

Remove from oven and let cool.

In the meantime, roast hazelnuts in the oven for about 10 minutes or until golden brown. Remove from oven and chop them roughly, along with apricots and dates.

When cool, combine everything, along with sultanas and wheat germ. You may store in air-tight container for up to one month.

Honey Butter with Cinnamon

Ingredients

- 1/2 cup honey
- 1/2 cup confectioners' sugar
- 1/2 cup butter, softened
- 1 tsp. ground cinnamon

Directions

Combine honey, confectioner's sugar, butter and cinnamon in a bowl. Beat until fluffy and light.

Ingredients

- 2 tbsp. honey
- 3 tbsp. minced garlic
- 1/4 cup soy sauce
- 1/2 cup balsamic vinegar
- 1/2 pound rib-eye steaks (2 pieces)
- 2 tbsp. olive oil
- 1 pinch cayenne pepper
- 1/2 tsp. liquid smoke flavoring
- 1/2 tsp. salt
- 1 tsp. onion powder
- 1 tsp. Worcestershire sauce
- 2 tsp. ground black pepper

Directions

Mix together honey, garlic, soy sauce, vinegar, liquid smoke, salt, onion powder, Worcestershire sauce, black pepper, olive oil, and cayenne pepper in a medium bowl.

Place the steak into the marinade and turn until well coated, rubbing the liquid into the steak. Marinate, covered, in the refrigerator for at least 24 hours.

Lightly grease the grate and preheat your grill to medium high heat. Grill the meat for about 7 minutes per side.

Ingredients

- 3/4 cup honey
- 2 eggs
- 1 cup vegetable oil
- 1 cup white sugar
- 3/4 cup chopped walnuts
- 3 peeled, cored and shredded apples
- 1/4 tsp. ground allspice
- 1 tsp. ground cinnamon
- 1 tsp. salt
- 1 tsp. baking soda
- 1 tsp. baking powder
- 2 1/2 cups all-purpose flour
- 1 tsp. vanilla extract

Directions

Preheat your oven to 325°F.Coat a 9-inch Bundt pan and lightly flour it.

Stir together oil and sugar in a large bowl. Whisk in the eggs, then stir in vanilla and honey.

In a small bowl, mix flour, allspice, cinnamon, salt, baking soda and baking powder. Stir the flour mixture into the batter and fold in nuts and apples.

Bake until a tester inserted in the center comes out clean, for about 65 minutes. Remove from oven and let cool for at least 15 minutes before transferring to a plate.

Ingredients

- 1 cup honey
- 1 cup plain flour
- 2 chicken breast fillet
- 1 tbsp. oil
- 1 cup water
- 1 tsp. ground black pepper
- 1 tsp. salt
- 1/2 cup sesame seeds, for garnishing

Directions

Chop your chicken into small pieces (bite size pieces).

Heat oil in a skillet set over medium heat; add chicken and cook until browned.

In a bowl, combine flour, salt and pepper; slowly whisk in water to form batter.

Roll the cooked chicken in batter, and then fry in hot oil until golden brown.

Heat honey in a small saucepan set over low heat until runny.

Drizzle the hot honey over chicken and sprinkle with sesame seeds.

Ingredients

- 1/3 cup blue gum honey
- 200g fresh reduced-fat ricotta
- 50g pine nuts
- 2 tbsp. mixed peel
- 8 fresh figs, halved

Directions

Set a frying pan over medium high heat. Add nuts and pine; cook until toasted, for about 2 minutes, stirring.

In a bowl, combine half of honey and ricotta.

Place the figs on plates and top with honey ricotta mixture; drizzle with the remaining honey and sprinkle with toasted nuts, pine and mixed peel. Enjoy!

Ingredients

- 1/4 cup honey
- 1 cup pitted prunes
- 50g butter, melted, cooled
- 2 1/2 cups toasted muesli
- 1/4 tsp. mixed spice

Directions

In a food processor, combine honey, prunes, 2 cups muesli, butter and mixed spice; process until well blended.

Place the remaining ½ cup of muesli on a plate. Roll 1 tablespoon of the honey mixture into a ball and roll in the muesli until well coated. Place the balls on a baking tray and refrigerate until firm, for about 30 minutes.

Keep the balls in airtight container in the refrigerator.

Ingredients

- 1/3 cup honey
- 600ml thickened cream
- 2 tsp. vanilla extract
- 1/3 cup caster sugar
- 4 egg yolks

Directions

In a saucepan set over medium heat, combine honey and cream; cook, stirring, for about 5 minutes and remove from heat.

Beat egg yolks, vanilla and sugar with an electric mixer in a bowl until creamy and thick. Slowly beat in the honey mixture until well blended. Transfer the mixture to a saucepan set over medium heat. Cook for about 15 minutes, stirring. Transfer to a rectangular cake pan and freeze, covered, until just firm, for about 3 hours.

Transfer to a large bowl and beat with an electric mixer until smooth. Pour the mixture into a loaf pan and freeze for about 6 hours. Serve.

Ingredients

- 1 1/2 tbsp. honey
- 125g wholegrain mustard
- 1 tbsp. mayonnaise

Directions

Whisk together honey, mustard and mayonnaise in a bowl until well mixed and creamy.

Serve the mustard with roast beef, rosemary and garlic.

Honey Mustard Dressing

Ingredients

- 2 tbsp. honey
- 1/3 cup mustard seed oil
- 1/2 cup apple cider vinegar
- 2 tbsp. wholegrain mustard

Directions

Combine honey, oil, vinegar and mustard in a bowl. Whisk with a fork until well blended. Season with ground pepper and salt.

Ingredients

- 1 tbsp. honey
- 1 tbsp. fresh lime juice
- 3 cups diced watermelon

Directions

In a food processor, blend together honey, lime juice and watermelon until smooth.

Pour the honey mixture into a bowl through a fine sieve.

Transfer the mixture to popsicle molds; freeze until solid to serve.

Ingredients

- 1 tbsp. honey
- 2 cups milk
- 2 cups frozen blueberries
- 2 cups natural vanilla ice cream

Directions

Combine all the ingredients in a blender and process until creamy and smooth. Serve immediately.

Ingredients

BASE:

- 4-5 tbsp. cold water
- 1½ cups oats, ground into flour
- 2 tbsp. coconut or oil
- 1 tbsp. coconut sugar
- ¼ t. sea salt

FILLING:

- 5 tbsp. raw honey
- 6 tbsp. lemon juice
- 1 tbsp. lemon zest
- 4 eggs
- scant ¼ tsp. powdered stevia extract
- ½ cups oats, ground into flour
- A pinch of sea salt

Directions

Preheat your oven to 350°F.

BASE:

Combine together coconut sugar, ground oats and salt. Stir in oil until pebbly.

Stir in water to form dough.

Press the dough in a greased 8 x 8 baking dish and bake for about 12 minutes.

Let cool as you prepare the filling.

FILLING:

In a bowl, beat the eggs with the remaining filling ingredients until smooth.

Pour the filling over the cooled crust and bake for about 20 minutes.

Let cool completely before cutting to serve.

COPYRIGHT

Author: Jason Miller

Publisher: Transcendence Publishing

Email: transpublishing@inbox.lv

Disclaimer